50 Cooking for Absolute Beginners Recipes

By: Kelly Johnson

Table of Contents

- Scrambled Eggs
- Boiled Eggs
- Fried Eggs
- Omelet
- Grilled Cheese Sandwich
- Peanut Butter & Jelly Sandwich
- Avocado Toast
- BLT Sandwich
- Tuna Salad Sandwich
- Egg Salad Sandwich
- Simple Pancakes
- French Toast
- Oatmeal
- Yogurt Parfait
- Banana Smoothie
- Basic Green Salad
- Caesar Salad
- Caprese Salad
- Cucumber & Tomato Salad
- Simple Stir-Fry (Chicken & Veggies)
- Pasta with Marinara Sauce
- Spaghetti Aglio e Olio
- Mac and Cheese
- Ramen with Egg
- Baked Potato
- Mashed Potatoes
- Roasted Vegetables
- Grilled Chicken Breast
- Baked Salmon
- Pan-Seared Steak
- Rice & Beans
- Garlic Butter Shrimp
- Simple Chili
- Chicken Noodle Soup
- Tomato Soup

- Vegetable Soup
- Baked Chicken Thighs
- Meatballs
- Sloppy Joes
- Tacos (Beef or Chicken)
- Quesadilla
- Guacamole
- Hummus
- Basic Fried Rice
- Hard Shell Tacos
- Simple Cheeseburger
- Hot Dog
- Baked Apples with Cinnamon
- Chocolate Mug Cake
- Fruit Salad

Fluffy Scrambled Eggs

Ingredients:

- 3 large eggs
- 2 tbsp milk or cream (optional, for creamier texture)
- 1 tbsp butter (or oil)
- Salt and pepper, to taste
- Optional: grated cheese, chopped herbs (chives, parsley), or a pinch of paprika

Instructions:

1. Whisk the eggs with milk/cream (if using), salt, and pepper until fully combined.
2. Heat a non-stick pan over low to medium heat and melt the butter.
3. Pour in the egg mixture and let it sit for a few seconds before gently stirring with a spatula.
4. Stir occasionally, pushing eggs from the edges toward the center, allowing soft curds to form.
5. Remove from heat when slightly underdone; the residual heat will finish cooking.
6. Serve immediately with desired toppings.

Boiled Eggs

Ingredients:

- 2–4 large eggs
- Water
- Ice (for cooling)

Instructions:

1. Place eggs in a saucepan and cover with water.
2. Bring to a boil, then reduce heat and simmer:
    - Soft-boiled: 6 minutes
    - Medium-boiled: 8–9 minutes
    - Hard-boiled: 10–12 minutes
3. Transfer eggs to an ice bath for 5 minutes before peeling.

Fried Eggs

Ingredients:

- 2 large eggs
- 1 tbsp butter or oil
- Salt and pepper, to taste

Instructions:

1. Heat butter or oil in a non-stick pan over medium heat.
2. Crack eggs into the pan and cook:
     - Sunny-side up: 2–3 minutes without flipping.
     - Over-easy: Flip and cook for 30 seconds.
     - Over-hard: Cook longer until yolk is firm.
3. Season and serve immediately.

Omelet

Ingredients:

- 3 large eggs
- 2 tbsp milk (optional)
- 1 tbsp butter
- Salt and pepper, to taste
- Fillings: cheese, vegetables, ham, herbs (optional)

Instructions:

1. Whisk eggs with milk, salt, and pepper.
2. Heat butter in a pan over medium-low heat.
3. Pour in eggs and let them set slightly before adding fillings.
4. Fold in half and cook until fully set.

Grilled Cheese Sandwich

Ingredients:

- 2 slices of bread
- 2 tbsp butter
- 2–3 slices of cheese (cheddar, American, or Swiss)

Instructions:

1. Butter one side of each bread slice.
2. Place one slice (butter-side down) in a pan over medium heat, add cheese, then top with the second slice (butter-side up).
3. Cook for 2–3 minutes per side until golden brown and cheese is melted.

Peanut Butter & Jelly Sandwich

Ingredients:

- 2 slices of bread
- 2 tbsp peanut butter
- 2 tbsp jelly or jam

Instructions:

1. Spread peanut butter on one slice and jelly on the other.
2. Press the slices together and serve.

Avocado Toast

Ingredients:

- 1 slice of bread (toasted)
- ½ ripe avocado
- Salt, pepper, and red pepper flakes (to taste)
- Optional toppings: egg, feta, tomato, smoked salmon

Instructions:

1. Mash avocado and spread it on toast.
2. Season with salt, pepper, and red pepper flakes.
3. Add optional toppings as desired.

BLT Sandwich

Ingredients:

- 2 slices of bread
- 3 slices of bacon
- 2 lettuce leaves
- 2 tomato slices
- 1 tbsp mayonnaise

Instructions:

1. Cook bacon until crispy.
2. Toast bread and spread with mayonnaise.
3. Layer lettuce, tomato, and bacon before serving.

Tuna Salad Sandwich

Ingredients:

- 1 can of tuna (drained)
- 2 tbsp mayonnaise
- 1 tbsp diced celery or onion (optional)
- Salt and pepper, to taste
- 2 slices of bread

Instructions:

1. Mix tuna, mayonnaise, celery/onion, salt, and pepper.
2. Spread mixture onto one slice of bread and top with another.

Egg Salad Sandwich

Ingredients:

- 2 hard-boiled eggs (chopped)
- 2 tbsp mayonnaise
- 1 tsp mustard
- Salt and pepper, to taste
- 2 slices of bread

Instructions:

1. Mix eggs, mayonnaise, mustard, salt, and pepper.
2. Spread onto one slice of bread and top with another.

Simple Pancakes

Ingredients:

- 1 cup flour
- 1 tbsp sugar
- 1 tsp baking powder
- 1 cup milk
- 1 egg
- 1 tbsp melted butter
- 1 tsp vanilla extract (optional)

Instructions:

1. Whisk together dry ingredients in a bowl.
2. In another bowl, whisk milk, egg, butter, and vanilla.
3. Combine wet and dry ingredients, mixing until just combined.
4. Heat a pan over medium heat and grease lightly.
5. Pour batter in small circles and cook until bubbles form, then flip and cook until golden.

French Toast

Ingredients:

- 2 slices of bread
- 2 eggs
- ½ cup milk
- 1 tsp vanilla extract
- ½ tsp cinnamon
- Butter for cooking
- Maple syrup and powdered sugar (for serving)

Instructions:

1. Whisk eggs, milk, vanilla, and cinnamon in a shallow bowl.
2. Dip each slice of bread in the mixture, coating both sides.
3. Heat butter in a pan over medium heat and cook bread for 2–3 minutes per sice until golden brown.
4. Serve with syrup and powdered sugar.

Oatmeal

Ingredients:

- ½ cup rolled oats
- 1 cup water or milk
- 1 tbsp honey or maple syrup
- Optional toppings: fruit, nuts, cinnamon

Instructions:

1. Bring water/milk to a boil and stir in oats.
2. Reduce heat and simmer for 5 minutes, stirring occasionally.
3. Sweeten and add toppings before serving.

Yogurt Parfait

Ingredients:

- 1 cup Greek yogurt
- ½ cup granola
- ½ cup mixed berries
- 1 tbsp honey (optional)

Instructions:

1. Layer yogurt, granola, and berries in a glass or bowl.
2. Drizzle with honey if desired.

Banana Smoothie

Ingredients:

- 1 banana
- 1 cup milk or yogurt
- 1 tbsp honey (optional)
- Ice cubes (optional)

Instructions:

1. Blend all ingredients until smooth.

Basic Green Salad

Ingredients:

- 2 cups mixed greens
- ½ cup cherry tomatoes (halved)
- ¼ cup sliced cucumber
- 2 tbsp olive oil
- 1 tbsp balsamic vinegar
- Salt and pepper, to taste

Instructions:

1. Toss greens, tomatoes, and cucumber in a bowl.
2. Drizzle with olive oil and balsamic vinegar.
3. Season and serve.

Caesar Salad

Ingredients:

- 2 cups romaine lettuce (chopped)
- ¼ cup grated Parmesan cheese
- ½ cup croutons
- 2 tbsp Caesar dressing

Instructions:

1. Toss lettuce, Parmesan, and croutons in a bowl.
2. Drizzle with dressing and mix well.

Caprese Salad

Ingredients:

- 2 large tomatoes (sliced)
- 1 ball fresh mozzarella (sliced)
- Fresh basil leaves
- 2 tbsp olive oil
- Salt and pepper, to taste

Instructions:

1. Layer tomato, mozzarella, and basil slices.
2. Drizzle with olive oil and season.

Cucumber & Tomato Salad

Ingredients:

- 1 cucumber (sliced)
- 1 cup cherry tomatoes (halved)
- ¼ red onion (sliced)
- 2 tbsp olive oil
- 1 tbsp lemon juice
- Salt and pepper, to taste

Instructions:

1. Toss cucumber, tomatoes, and onion in a bowl.
2. Drizzle with olive oil and lemon juice.
3. Season and serve.

Simple Stir-Fry (Chicken & Veggies)

Ingredients:

- 1 chicken breast (sliced)
- 1 cup mixed vegetables (bell peppers, carrots, broccoli)
- 1 tbsp soy sauce
- 1 tbsp olive oil
- 1 tsp garlic (minced)

Instructions:

1. Heat oil in a pan over medium-high heat.
2. Cook chicken until browned, then add garlic and vegetables.
3. Stir-fry for 5 minutes, add soy sauce, and cook for 1 more minute.

Pasta with Marinara Sauce

Ingredients:

- 8 oz pasta
- 1 cup marinara sauce
- 1 tbsp olive oil
- 1 clove garlic (minced)
- Grated Parmesan cheese (for serving)

Instructions:

1. Cook pasta according to package instructions.
2. Heat olive oil in a pan, sauté garlic, then add marinara sauce.
3. Simmer for 5 minutes, then toss with pasta.
4. Serve with Parmesan cheese.

Spaghetti Aglio e Olio

Ingredients:

- 8 oz spaghetti
- ¼ cup olive oil
- 4 cloves garlic (sliced)
- ½ tsp red pepper flakes
- ¼ cup chopped parsley
- Salt and Parmesan cheese (for serving)

Instructions:

1. Cook spaghetti and reserve ½ cup pasta water.
2. Heat olive oil in a pan, sauté garlic and red pepper flakes.
3. Toss in cooked spaghetti and pasta water.
4. Stir in parsley and serve with Parmesan.

Mac and Cheese

Ingredients:

- 8 oz elbow macaroni
- 2 tbsp butter
- 2 tbsp flour
- 1 cup milk
- 1½ cups shredded cheddar cheese
- Salt and pepper, to taste

Instructions:

1. Cook macaroni according to package instructions.
2. In a saucepan, melt butter, stir in flour, and cook for 1 minute.
3. Slowly whisk in milk, cook until thickened, then stir in cheese.
4. Mix in cooked macaroni and serve.

Ramen with Egg

Ingredients:

- 1 pack instant ramen
- 2 cups water
- 1 egg
- ½ tsp soy sauce (optional)
- ½ green onion (sliced, optional)

Instructions:

1. Cook ramen noodles in boiling water.
2. Crack an egg into the pot and let it poach for 2–3 minutes.
3. Stir in seasoning, add soy sauce, and top with green onion.

Baked Potato

Ingredients:

- 1 large russet potato
- 1 tbsp olive oil
- Salt, to taste
- Butter, sour cream, cheese (optional toppings)

Instructions:

1. Preheat oven to 400°F (200°C).
2. Rub potato with oil and salt, then pierce with a fork.
3. Bake for 45–60 minutes until soft inside.
4. Slice open and add toppings.

Mashed Potatoes

Ingredients:

- 4 large potatoes (peeled and cubed)
- ½ cup milk
- 4 tbsp butter
- Salt and pepper, to taste

Instructions:

1. Boil potatoes until fork-tender, then drain.
2. Mash with butter and milk until smooth.
3. Season and serve.

Roasted Vegetables

Ingredients:

- 2 cups mixed vegetables (carrots, bell peppers, zucchini)
- 2 tbsp olive oil
- ½ tsp salt
- ½ tsp black pepper
- ½ tsp garlic powder

Instructions:

1. Preheat oven to 400°F (200°C).
2. Toss vegetables with oil and seasonings.
3. Spread on a baking sheet and roast for 20–25 minutes.

Grilled Chicken Breast

Ingredients:

- 1 chicken breast
- 1 tbsp olive oil
- ½ tsp salt
- ½ tsp black pepper
- ½ tsp garlic powder

Instructions:

1. Preheat grill to medium heat.
2. Rub chicken with oil and seasonings.
3. Grill for 5–7 minutes per side until fully cooked.

Baked Salmon

Ingredients:

- 1 salmon fillet
- 1 tbsp olive oil
- ½ tsp salt
- ½ tsp black pepper
- 1 lemon wedge

Instructions:

1. Preheat oven to 400°F (200°C).
2. Place salmon on a baking sheet, drizzle with oil, and season.
3. Bake for 12–15 minutes, then serve with lemon.

Pan-Seared Steak

Ingredients:

- 1 steak (ribeye, sirloin, or filet mignon)
- 1 tbsp butter
- ½ tsp salt
- ½ tsp black pepper
- 2 garlic cloves (crushed, optional)

Instructions:

1. Season steak with salt and pepper.
2. Heat a skillet over high heat and sear steak for 3–5 minutes per side.
3. Add butter and garlic, baste steak, then let it rest before serving.

Rice & Beans

Ingredients:

- 1 cup rice
- 1 cup canned beans (black or pinto, drained)
- 1 tbsp olive oil
- 1 garlic clove (minced)
- ½ tsp salt

Instructions:

1. Cook rice according to package instructions.
2. Heat oil in a pan, sauté garlic, then stir in beans.
3. Combine with rice and season.

Garlic Butter Shrimp

Ingredients:

- ½ lb shrimp (peeled and deveined)
- 2 tbsp butter
- 2 garlic cloves (minced)
- ½ tsp salt
- ½ tsp red pepper flakes (optional)

Instructions:

1. Heat butter in a pan over medium heat.
2. Add garlic and shrimp, cooking for 2–3 minutes per side.
3. Season and serve immediately.

Simple Chili

Ingredients:

- 1 lb ground beef
- 1 can (15 oz) kidney beans (drained)
- 1 can (15 oz) diced tomatoes
- 1 tbsp chili powder
- ½ tsp salt

Instructions:

1. Brown ground beef in a pot over medium heat.
2. Stir in beans, tomatoes, chili powder, and salt.
3. Simmer for 20 minutes, then serve.

Chicken Noodle Soup

Ingredients:

- 1 tbsp olive oil
- 1 small onion (chopped)
- 2 carrots (sliced)
- 2 celery stalks (sliced)
- 2 garlic cloves (minced)
- 4 cups chicken broth
- 1 cup shredded cooked chicken
- 1 cup egg noodles
- Salt and pepper, to taste

Instructions:

1. Heat olive oil in a pot over medium heat. Sauté onion, carrots, celery, and garlic for 5 minutes.
2. Add chicken broth and bring to a boil.
3. Stir in chicken and noodles, then simmer for 10 minutes until noodles are tender.
4. Season and serve.

Tomato Soup

Ingredients:

- 1 tbsp olive oil
- 1 small onion (chopped)
- 2 garlic cloves (minced)
- 1 can (28 oz) crushed tomatoes
- 2 cups vegetable broth
- ½ tsp salt
- ½ cup heavy cream (optional)

Instructions:

1. Heat olive oil in a pot over medium heat. Sauté onion and garlic until soft.
2. Add crushed tomatoes, broth, and salt. Simmer for 15 minutes.
3. Blend until smooth, stir in cream (if using), and serve.

Vegetable Soup

Ingredients:

- 1 tbsp olive oil
- 1 onion (chopped)
- 2 carrots (sliced)
- 2 celery stalks (sliced)
- 1 can (14 oz) diced tomatoes
- 4 cups vegetable broth
- 1 cup mixed vegetables (peas, green beans, corn)
- Salt and pepper, to taste

Instructions:

1. Heat olive oil in a pot over medium heat. Sauté onion, carrots, and celery.
2. Add tomatoes, broth, and mixed vegetables. Simmer for 20 minutes.
3. Season and serve.

Baked Chicken Thighs

Ingredients:

- 4 bone-in, skin-on chicken thighs
- 1 tbsp olive oil
- ½ tsp salt
- ½ tsp black pepper
- ½ tsp garlic powder

Instructions:

1. Preheat oven to 400°F (200°C).
2. Rub chicken with oil and seasonings.
3. Bake for 35–40 minutes until crispy and cooked through.

Meatballs

Ingredients:

- 1 lb ground beef
- ½ cup breadcrumbs
- 1 egg
- 1 tsp garlic powder
- ½ tsp salt
- ½ tsp black pepper

Instructions:

1. Preheat oven to 375°F (190°C).
2. Mix all ingredients and form into meatballs.
3. Bake for 20 minutes or pan-fry until browned.

Sloppy Joes

Ingredients:

- 1 lb ground beef
- ½ small onion (chopped)
- 1 cup tomato sauce
- 1 tbsp Worcestershire sauce
- 1 tbsp brown sugar
- 4 hamburger buns

Instructions:

1. Brown ground beef and onion in a pan.
2. Stir in tomato sauce, Worcestershire sauce, and sugar. Simmer for 10 minutes.
3. Serve on buns.

Tacos (Beef or Chicken)

Ingredients:

- 1 lb ground beef or shredded cooked chicken
- 1 tbsp taco seasoning
- ½ cup water
- 8 small tortillas
- Toppings: lettuce, cheese, salsa, sour cream

Instructions:

1. Cook beef or chicken in a pan over medium heat.
2. Add taco seasoning and water, simmer for 5 minutes.
3. Serve in tortillas with toppings.

Quesadilla

Ingredients:

- 2 large flour tortillas
- 1 cup shredded cheese (cheddar, Monterey Jack)
- ½ cup cooked chicken or vegetables (optional)
- 1 tbsp butter

Instructions:

1. Heat butter in a pan over medium heat.
2. Place one tortilla in the pan, sprinkle with cheese and filling, then top with the second tortilla.
3. Cook for 2–3 minutes per side until golden. Slice and serve.

Guacamole

Ingredients:

- 2 ripe avocados
- 1 small tomato (diced)
- ¼ red onion (finely chopped)
- 1 tbsp lime juice
- ½ tsp salt

Instructions:

1. Mash avocados in a bowl.
2. Stir in tomato, onion, lime juice, and salt.

Hummus

Ingredients:

- 1 can (15 oz) chickpeas (drained)
- 2 tbsp tahini
- 2 tbsp olive oil
- 1 clove garlic
- 1 tbsp lemon juice
- ½ tsp salt

Instructions:

1. Blend all ingredients until smooth.

Basic Fried Rice

Ingredients:

- 2 cups cooked rice (cold)
- 1 tbsp vegetable oil
- ½ cup mixed vegetables (peas, carrots, corn)
- 2 eggs (beaten)
- 1 tbsp soy sauce

Instructions:

1. Heat oil in a pan over medium heat.
2. Sauté vegetables for 2 minutes, then push to the side and scramble eggs.
3. Stir in rice and soy sauce, cook for 3 more minutes.

Hard Shell Tacos

Ingredients:

- 1 lb ground beef
- 1 tbsp taco seasoning
- ½ cup water
- 8 hard taco shells
- Toppings: lettuce, cheese, salsa

Instructions:

1. Cook beef in a pan over medium heat.
2. Add taco seasoning and water, simmer for 5 minutes.
3. Fill hard taco shells with beef and toppings.

Simple Cheeseburger

Ingredients:

- 1 lb ground beef
- ½ tsp salt
- ½ tsp black pepper
- 4 hamburger buns
- 4 slices cheese (cheddar, American, or Swiss)
- Toppings: lettuce, tomato, pickles, ketchup, mustard

Instructions:

1. Form beef into 4 patties, season with salt and pepper.
2. Cook patties in a skillet over medium heat for 3–4 minutes per side.
3. Place cheese on top of patties and cover until melted.
4. Assemble burgers with buns and toppings.

Hot Dog

Ingredients:

- 4 hot dog buns
- 4 hot dogs
- Optional toppings: mustard, ketchup, relish, onions

Instructions:

1. Boil, grill, or pan-fry hot dogs until heated through.
2. Place in buns and add desired toppings.

Baked Apples with Cinnamon

Ingredients:

- 2 apples (sliced)
- 1 tbsp brown sugar
- ½ tsp cinnamon
- 1 tbsp butter (melted)

Instructions:

1. Preheat oven to 375°F (190°C).
2. Toss apple slices with brown sugar, cinnamon, and melted butter.
3. Bake for 20 minutes until tender.

Chocolate Mug Cake

Ingredients:

- 4 tbsp flour
- 2 tbsp sugar
- 2 tbsp cocoa powder
- ¼ tsp baking powder
- 3 tbsp milk
- 2 tbsp vegetable oil
- ¼ tsp vanilla extract

Instructions:

1. Mix all ingredients in a microwave-safe mug.
2. Microwave for 1 minute or until set.

Fruit Salad

Ingredients:

- 1 cup strawberries (sliced)
- 1 cup grapes (halved)
- 1 banana (sliced)
- 1 apple (diced)
- 1 tbsp honey or orange juice (optional)

Instructions:

1. Combine all fruit in a bowl.
2. Drizzle with honey or orange juice if desired.

www.ingramcontent.com/pod-product-compliance
Lightning Source LLC
LaVergne TN
LVHW061954070526
838199LV00060B/4105